THE SIMPLE SHIFT: SMALL CHANGES, BIG RESULTS

Table of Contents

The SIMPLE Shift Method _____ *6*
See the Challenge _____ *10*
Identify Tools and Resources _____ *19*
Make a Plan _____ *26*
Practice Consistently _____ *33*
Learn and Adjust _____ *40*
Evolve Continuously _____ *46*
The Power of the SIMPLE Shift _____ *51*
The Simple Shift Method in Action _____ 59
Acknowledgements _____ 66

Dedication

This book is dedicated to my children, Trey and Brooklynn. I pray that you overcome every obstacle that is set in your way throughout life. From learning to use your words, to tying your shoes, to emotional maturity, to healthy friendships, to marriage and parenthood. You deserve every good thing, and you are equipped for every "not good" thing. I love you. Go live the life you want to live……simply because you can.

Introduction

The SIMPLE Shift Method

"You don't have to stay stuck. You got options."

– Rafer Owens, Jr.

What's up? I'm Rafer Owens, Jr., a certified life coach, master mindset coach, and the creator of the **Simple Shift Method**—a step-by-step framework designed to help people create lasting change through small, intentional actions. With years of experience coaching individuals to overcome challenges and unlock their potential, I've seen firsthand how even the smallest shifts can lead to incredible transformation. The Simple Shift Method was born out of my passion for making growth accessible and effective for anyone ready to take control of their life. Unlike programs that demand an immediate overhaul, the Simple Shift Method works with your reality, not against it—one simple shift at a time.

The Simple Shift Method is a six-step process summarized by the acronym SIMPLE:

- **See the Challenge**: Build awareness of where you are and where you want to go.

- **Identify Tools and Resources**: Find what you need to get where you want to be.
- **Make a Plan**: Create an actionable, manageable plan that you can follow daily.
- **Practice Consistently**: Show up every day, regardless of how you feel. Consistency is where the magic happens.
- **Learn and Adjust**: Evaluate what's working, tweak what isn't, and keep moving forward. The goal stays the same, but the method can change.
- **Evolve Continuously**: Keep learning, gaining knowledge, and growing. Life doesn't stop, and neither should your progress.

For many people, the idea of changing their lives feels overwhelming. It's too much to tackle at once. The Simple Shift Method provides a clear, concise path to achieve the things you want in life. But here's the catch: Every goal, dream, or wish you have is ultimately a battle against yourself. The challenge isn't just external; it's internal. Whether it's emotional intelligence, finances, or physical and mental goals, the SSM is here to help you overcome the real obstacle—you. And it does so by breaking things down into small, intentional steps you can take every day.

Why Small, Intentional Steps?

The answer is simple: life is already complex. The world is complex. People are different, they respond differently, and some days you feel great, while other days, you don't. All this complexity can make change seem insurmountable. That's why the Simple Shift Method works—it turns mountains into manageable steps.

Here's an example: My wife and I paid off $54,016 of debt in one year. A massive feat, right? But the most important thing we could do on any given day was stick to the budget. We broke the big goal into smaller plans. First, we created a yearly goal. That led to monthly budgets. Then bi-weekly budgets. And finally, daily tasks. Each day, we woke up, checked the bank account, and compared it to our budget and debt payoff goals. Then we acted accordingly. That's what it took—simple steps, executed daily.

This story, which I'll revisit throughout this book, was the catalyst for this process. Before our debt payoff journey, I was an emotional spender. If I had a hard day, I spent money. If I wanted something, I bought it. Meanwhile, my wife felt like we were perpetually broke. We fought constantly about money. The breaking point came when she asked if it was okay to buy shoes for our children. At that moment, I felt like a failure—as though I had let her down. That conversation made me realize I needed to change, not just in my budgeting skills but in myself.

The Birth of the Simple Shift Method

As we tackled our debt, the Simple Shift Method began to take shape naturally. And as our finances improved, I started to look at other areas of my life that needed attention—my marriage, emotional health, physical health, business, parenting, and even this book! What began as a strategy for financial challenges became a framework that transformed every area of my life.

Over the years, by applying this method slowly and intentionally, my life changed drastically. Now, I want to share this gift with you.

What to Expect from This Book

Simplicity. Practical how-to's. Encouragement that goes beyond compare.

Life can feel isolating, but you're not alone. Everything in this book has been tested in real life—by me, my friends, my coworkers, and my family. One thing I've learned is that, despite life's complexities, we're all more alike than we realize. My goal is to help you become the person you want to be, free of self-imposed limitations and expectations.

As you read, think about a hurdle in your life that feels too big. This book will guide you step by step to overcome it. By the end, you won't just believe change is possible—you'll know how to make it happen.

Cheers to a life you want to live. Are you ready? Let's get started!

CHAPTER 1

See the Challenge

"Awareness is the first step toward change. You can't fix what you don't see." - Anonymous

---

One Saturday morning, I realized something shocking: I didn't like my 6-year-old son as a person.

I know what you're thinking, "what? That's crazy! Who says that about their kid?"

I did. And it was a very telling moment for me. If anyone in my life, including my wife, had told you what kind of father I was, their words would have been nothing but great. I was passing every mark for what society would have described as a "good dad": present, playful, encouraging, calm (most of the time lol), thoughtful, teacher, etc. I was killing the game. But in my heart, I knew what I felt and what I thought.

I knew that I disciplined my son differently than my daughter. I knew I was tougher on him than I was on her. And it wasn't because he was older. It wasn't because he knew more than she did. It was simply because I didn't like the person my son was becoming. As I began to unpack this jarring thought I had on my Saturday morning walk, it was heartbreaking to come to the realization of the statement.

I began to ask myself questions about what I felt. "Why don't you like him?" "How has that affected your relationship with him?" "Do you think he knows or has felt it?" "Have you jacked him up for the rest of his life?"

My mind was spinning, and I couldn't slow it down. And then it hit me, "Answer the first question and go from there." As I answered the first question (why don't you like him?) I realized my son was my bro. He was my hangout buddy. And up until this point, he had done pretty much whatever I wanted him to do. He repeated things I said and did. He sounded like me. He acted like me. And during his 6th year of life, he was becoming himself. And while that was ok, I had started to treat him like an adult friend of mine. I didn't like the way he did certain things. I didn't like how he processed things. I didn't like his word choice. I realized that I wanted, and expected, him to keep being who I wanted him to be.

My little boy was becoming himself and the problem wasn't with him, it was with my expectations of him. As I looked at how I treated him because of this, I became filled with guilt, shame and sorrow. I knew I needed to make it right with him and I needed to change. All of this was possible because I decided to become aware of my thoughts and actions.

Why Awareness Matters

In any given process, awareness is the very first step. Further, you need awareness in every step along the way. What is awareness? Awareness is a state of having knowledge; to be conscious; cognizant; informed; alert; knowledgeable of something. Awareness isn't just the first step in SIMPLE–it's the thread that runs through every step, guiding you toward the life you want.

When it comes to life, your goals, the person you want to become, you must have this information. You must have the knowledge of where you are and where you want to go. It is simply having the knowledge about yourself.

I've done quite a bit of coaching over the last few years. So many people struggle with finances, emotional intelligence, and relationships (with themselves or otherwise). A lot of these issues stem from childhood and early adulthood. The problem is not that we all have issues, the problem is that we are not aware of the issues so that they can be addressed and moved on from.

Facing the Truth

"I don't want to be self-aware because I don't want to be selfish". This was said to me in a marriage counseling session. I was explaining this very topic and the benefits of becoming self-aware. Simply knowing yourself. Why do you respond to things the way you do? Knowing what makes you tick. Having information about yourself so that it could be shared with your spouse. And this

person wanted no part of it because they "didn't want to be selfish". What they didn't realize was in taking that stance, they kept themselves locked into unhealthy cycles and patterns that were no longer serving them.

Trust me, I completely understand how hard this may be at first. It can even be scary. but here's the thing, you can't fix what you can't see. Awareness isn't about judgment, it's about freedom. There are 2 big things that happen when we avoid building awareness and seeing the challenge that is us.

Breaking the Unhealthy Cycles

First, we stay locked into unhealthy cycles and patterns that no longer serve us. We continue to shut people out when they're genuinely trying to learn more about us. We spend money when we're angry to feel some sense of control. We manipulate others into doing what we want them to do because that's what we've always done. That's what was happening with myself and my son. I was used to relating to him in a specific way and vice versa. It was starting to cause friction between the two of us. When I took the time to gather information about what I felt, I was able to move forward. And it's the same in all those scenarios. If we take the time to gather information about ourselves, we can react and move differently.

Another thing that happens when you avoid awareness is you spiral quickly. When you don't know where you are or where you want to go, in any facet of life, you spiral. This can be emotionally, relationally, financially, physically. Think about a GPS as it's planning your route out of a parking garage. It knows where you want to go, but it can't find where you are. So, the icon that represents you spins and spins and spins. You turn one way, and it finally sets on the path only for you to turn again and it begins to spin again. This is what we do when we lack awareness. Everything is a great idea. Every plan seems like it will work. Every book is the best book. Every TikTok has the best information. But because we don't know where we're going OR we don't know where we are, we spin and spiral under the pressure of so many options in front of us and choose nothing. Then we revert to the same patterns and cycles.

Building Awareness: 4 Steps

Learning to build awareness is, again, a very simple step to take. When we look at building awareness as gathering information, it becomes easier to lean into that process. Like the client above, many people stay stuck for years! And it isn't because they can't change, but because they never stop to ask what's going on. They never stop to check in on themselves. Awareness opens the door to everything else. So how do you build awareness?

Awareness is built in 4 steps:

1) Take notice of what's happening: in the room, in your mind, in your body

2) Ask yourself what's going on
3) Ask yourself why you feel the way you do
4) Ask yourself what you want in this situation

TAKE NOTICE
Heart rate: does it speed up in specific moments? When I need to make a decision? When I talk to my spouse about a certain topic? When I become overwhelmed making plans? When I want to start something new? The list goes on.

Racing thoughts: Do my thoughts make sense? Can I keep up?

Temperament: Am I quiet when I'm normally not? Am I talking a lot when I normally don't? Am I speaking too quickly? Am I unnecessarily angry? Am I being fake nice?

Body: Am I clenching my jaw? My fists? How's my posture?

All these things can let us know when something's up. Each of these parts have many more examples of what may take place in our minds and bodies. It's up to us to slow down and begin to gather information about what's happening.

WHAT'S GOING ON?
This leads to the next step of the awareness process: Being honest. You must tell yourself the truth. A lot of the time we stay away from the truth of what we feel because of the shame we've been made to carry for our feelings. But feelings are just that: feelings. You must begin to practice giving yourself the freedom and grace to explore

those wild and crazy thoughts. It's the only way you can build real awareness of where you are. So even if the answer is, "I don't like my son. Like, as a person." The only way that thought pattern can change is by naming it honestly.

WHY DO I FEEL THIS WAY?
Again, honesty really is the best policy in these circumstances. Majority of the time it comes down to a simple explanation. For me, I was treating my son like an annoying 30-year-old who needed too much attention that I didn't have to give. I know, very harsh to say aloud. But it was the truth. And in having that truth, I was able to change the expectations I had for him, myself and our relationship. As you answer these questions honestly, there's a freedom that will come because you can finally express what you feel.

WHAT DO I ACTUALLY WANT?
Asking yourself what you want or who you want to be is a game changer. It takes the focus from what's wrong and not going well to hope. Hope of what can be. Hope for who we can become. It's a simple question, but a very hard question to ask: What do I want? Who do I want to become? It may take some time to come to a complete answer, but if you can start thinking about what your future could look like in every circumstance, your life can become whatever you want it to be.

There are multiple ways to work this process too! You can journal, voice record, talk to a friend, sit with a therapist or life coach. My favorite way to process is to walk and talk out loud. I love being outside and walking through my problems. I ask myself these very questions and just talk them out. I like to bounce things off the Holy Spirit. Sometimes He answers, sometimes He lets me arrive at things on my own. Either way, I'm purposefully walking this awareness process.

That Saturday morning, I realized how much my "dislike" for my son was hindering the relationship I wanted to have with him. By noticing that my heart rate was going up when I was talking to him. Or noticing the feeling I had in my body when I had to discipline him and how it was different from my daughter. I realized something wasn't ok. I took a walk and pointed those things out to myself. I asked myself what was going on in those moments. I asked myself why I felt that way. And when I got to the final question of what I wanted in this situation, my answer surprised me. I wanted to be a better dad. I wanted to enjoy my son and our relationship. I wanted to be a man that he felt safe with. I wanted to laugh with him. I wanted to be his bro on a level that he wanted. I wanted a high-quality relationship with my 6yr old in my heart and mind. And that changed everything for me and him. I went and explained, in 6yr old terms, where I had been and how I wanted to be better for him. I apologized for being mean. The best part of this was his response when I asked him if he felt like I had been mean to him. He said, "Yeah. Sometimes. Like you don't let me wear my skate shoes in the house with the lights on them." It was at that moment that I realized that he's still six. He's still a little boy. And his life isn't as complex as mine. I still had a chance to be a better dad than I had been. And it all came from seeing this challenge in front of me. I built some awareness, and this part of my life changed for the better.

That's the point of Seeing the Challenge. We must give ourselves the room to gather information about ourselves. We must find out where we are and where we want to go. Sometimes those answers are terribly hard things to say. Sometimes they're easy to navigate. No matter what, keep learning about yourself. It will always be uncomfortable. Every time. The comfortability gets easier to deal with the more you practice seeing the challenge (yourself) for what it is. Awareness is worth the discomfort because things will be way better on the other side. At this moment you can't even imagine how great they can be. But very quickly you will see how much it's worth.

At the end of the day, the question I raise to you is this: do you want to continue spinning or do you want to get to the destination you put into the GPS?

The choice is yours and yours alone. No one can make you do anything. You must want something different for yourself. And if you want something different for yourself, you must know 2 things: 1) where you are currently, and 2) where you want to go.

Take 10 minutes today to sit quietly and ask yourself: what's going on? Why do I feel this way? What do I want? Write down your answers. This small step is the start of something big.

You can do it. The life you want is the life you deserve. The rest of the journey awaits you in the following chapters.

CHAPTER 2

Identify Tools and Resources

"The tools you need for success are all around you; it's just a matter of recognizing them." - Zig Ziglar

---

I was sitting in a fellowship hall at a church in a small town in Texas. There was a gentleman in his mid-fifties giving a talk. About what? I don't remember. But what I do remember is looking around the room at all these older men crying. And while what was being said was very heartfelt and emotional, I couldn't cry. I wanted to cry. But I just couldn't do it. My mind began to wander in that meeting that day. I started thinking about my father and how rarely I had seen him cry and how when we talk about my children, his grandchildren, he will begin to tear up. I thought about all these men I sat in this room with, they're so openly emotional and they haven't always been this way. It was mind-boggling to me how much I watched these men change over the years. Specifically, regarding crying. I told God I didn't want to wait until I was in my fifties to cry. I wanted to be emotionally available now, with my wife, my kids, my friends, my family. I wanted it at that moment. While I was aware of where I was and where I wanted to go, the process had just started on how to get there.

The Role of Tools in Transformation

The next part of the SIMPLE Shift Method is I – Identify Tools and Resources. While most people will tell you to get a goal and make a plan to get there, I like to prepare for the journey ahead, so I know HOW to plan. And that's what this step is all about: finding the things you are going to need for the journey itself.

After seeing a challenge (knowing where you are and where you want to go), the best thing you can do is find tools and resources to help you get there. This is a very important step because up to this point, you've been operating in a certain way that may not serve you anymore. I like to look at this step like clearing out a house so you can renovate. You have an idea of what you want the house to look like. You have an idea of how it should feel when you walk in. But to get to that point, you need to have conversations with people who have been there before. You need pointers and tools and best practices so that you can properly and efficiently renovate your home. Your life, your mind, your finances, your emotional health are 'the home'. And to get where you want to go in each of these areas, you must gain some knowledge to make a plan that will best fit you.

Internal and External Tools and Resources

Both internal and external tools that are going to help you on your journey.

Internal tools and resources are things like your mindset, resilience, habits, confidence, motivation, and self-discipline. All these things develop as you make your way through your journey. These things all take a bit of new data to grow. When starting a journey to change your life, many people think the internal resources and tools should develop quickly. Or they assume something is wrong with them because these things don't develop quickly. And while it does take time for them to develop, they are very important and vital to your overall success. Depending on them too early will, unfortunately, kill your momentum and success. At the beginning of your journey, you must lean on external tools and resources.

External tools and resources are abundant! Books, coaches, social media pages, YouTube, podcasts, etc. There are so many options out there for every type of learner. The fact that you're reading this book makes that point! However you best process information, there's a resource for it. Find a mentor or a coach. Talk to friends that have done what you're aiming for. Going back to our renovation example, when you have someone that's done it before or is doing what you want to do, there's so much information you can glean from them without experiencing as many pitfalls yourself. Now, this does not mean that you will pick information from their brains and immediately have success. It does not mean you won't have any pitfalls or hiccups yourself. It does mean that you have more knowledge for what's to come and can better plan for those things because of this knowledge. Free knowledge is the best knowledge. We'll talk about what to do with this knowledge in the following chapters.

How does one assess what tools they currently have, if any? As I said earlier in this chapter, you've been operating a certain way in every area of your life up to this point. You have to use that awareness tool to get to the reality of where you currently are and what's serving you.

There are 3 steps that help us assess what tools we currently have: Awareness, naming my issue, naming my coping behaviors.

Practical Steps to Identify Your Tools
In many cases, we've operated like this for so long, we don't know there's a faulty toolbelt hurting us more than it's helping. In every area of your life, once you know where you want to go, you must take a real thorough look at your life and analyze how you respond to people and different situations. Again, it may feel like second nature so you may miss it at first glance. For years I had seen people cry at different moments. Both tears of joy and sadness. I wanted to feel that. I knew something was missing because I didn't have what they had. Awareness was the first step in the process of assessing my current tools.

Second, I named what my issue was. In being able to name your problem, it allows you to directly change that line of thought and, further, the behavior. I lacked emotional intelligence. I couldn't name any emotions I had. I couldn't allow myself to feel. I didn't use emotional words. I didn't have a list to pull from if I wanted to! But being able to see that I was emotionally unavailable and naming it, changed everything for me.

Lastly, check your unhealthy emotional behaviors. I started to look at how I coped in situations I didn't like. Or how I responded to people I didn't get along with. I noticed I would get angry quickly and shut down. With my wife, my kids, and my friends. I just shut completely off. Even with clients. It I felt as if I wasn't being listened to, I'd get angry so fast! I learned very quickly that I coped and "protected" myself by becoming emotionally unavailable. It wasn't okay by any means. Come to find out, that was the driving force of why I couldn't cry; happy or sad.

Once I came to understand the "tools" I had been using and how they weren't serving me on the path I wanted to take, I began to look for new tools. I took an Interpersonal Communications class, I read countless books on emotional health and intelligence. I worked with a therapist. I found pages on Instagram that promoted emotional health and agility. I changed what I took in mindlessly on Instagram and TikTok. I talked to friends I trusted and allowed them to point me in a direction that helped me. Crazy enough, the beginning of the breakthrough came from a friend that said, "Google emotion words and start there". As I found words to describe what I felt, it changed me. I was able to walk a path that allowed me to open up emotionally like never before. Having emotional words helped me take responsibility for myself in my closest relationships. I learned I felt dismissed and was able to express that to them. I could name what I felt without getting angry. It allowed for deeper, healing conversations. All it took was having a new set of tools.

You may be thinking you don't have the right tools to succeed. I want you to know that is completely ok! Identifying what's missing is part of the process. As you saw, I was there. Sometimes the right tools don't appear until we're ready to look for them.

If you're saying to yourself, "I don't have a college class to take or a therapist to turn to", Google, ChatGPT, Podcasts, and YouTube are ALL FREE! Simply searching for what you're looking for will give you the edge you're looking for in your particular area of life. Emotional Intelligence, improving your finances, maintaining a healthy lifestyle, learning a new skill, your relationships, etc. The information is out there. It just needs to be found. In the next chapter we'll discuss what to do with all that information. For now, just start looking for things that you think can help you get to where you want to go. Stack the toolbelt. We'll discard unhelpful tools as we move forward.

Before we move on, take a few minutes to make two lists: What tools do you already have within yourself? What outside resources can you tap into? Don't overthink it - just start writing.

CHAPTER 3

Make a Plan

"A goal without a plan is just a wish."

— Antoine de Saint-Exupéry

You have awareness of where you are and where you want to go. You've started to gather new tools. You're listening to podcasts. You've revamped your TikTok algorithm. You've cleaned up your Instagram feed. You've started reading. What do you do with all of this? You make a plan.

Having a plan is vital to the process. Going back to our GPS analogy, every trip has a plan on how to get there. Without steps to take, a path to walk, or markers to hit, we will either stay overwhelmed with tools and resources or wander aimlessly. A good plan isn't just about action steps, it's about making sure those steps lead you closer to the life you truly want.

When my wife and I started our debt payoff journey, we had 7 debts that totaled $54,016. A car, a couple of credit cards, and multiple student loans. We were down bad. And as I said earlier, I knew I had bad money management skills. I knew I was an emotional spender. I knew my wife was having a hard time with my spending habits. With all of that, I knew I was going to get a massive raise at work and if I didn't have a plan for this influx of money, I was going to spend it; quickly. So, I sat down with my wife, and we made a plan.

A couple of years before this we had taken a Dave Ramsey course at our church. In that course, Dave presented the Baby Step Program. Steps 1 and 2 were all we ever got to: 1) Save $1000 as quickly as possible and 2) Pay your debt off as quickly as possible using the Debt Snowball Process. The Debt Snowball is when you take all your debts and pay them off from smallest to largest by the total amount owed. Ignore interest rate, just get wins by paying the debt off as fast as you can. This tends to work for most people because they get tangible results quickly and are more prone to stick to the program overall.

When we sat down to make our plan, neither of us wanted to have this conversation. We couldn't have a conversation about money without fighting. And when we fought, we wouldn't talk for a few days. It was much easier to not talk about it at all. With that being the situation, I knew that my current tools (financial, emotional, interpersonal) weren't helping me. So, I read Total Money Makeover by Dave Ramsey in July of 2020, took all ideas from that book and presented The Baby Step plan to my wife. Thankfully this Dave Ramsey plan involved little to no unnecessary spending and she quickly jumped on board. How did we do it? We took this massive amount of debt and broke it down into small, actionable steps we could handle every day.

Breaking Big Goals into Small Steps

Too often when we start a change in our lives, we overestimate how much we can do in a month and severely underestimate how much we can do in a year. It's just how our brains work. And due to technology, we want everything "right now" or as quickly as possible. This is why the SIMPLE Shift Method works the way it does; know where you're going, gather some tools, and build a plan to get there. You must start things slowly and intentionally. My favorite thing about making a plan, it only needs to work for you. You make the plan that best fits you, your personality, your way of learning. It can only work if it fits what YOU are capable of doing.

There are multiple ways to build a plan. Here are a few of my personal favorites: Ceiling/Floor goals, SMART goals, and Systems/Habit based.

CEILING/FLOOR Goals

There's an idea floating around the internet that I love, "have a ceiling and have a floor". A Ceiling action is the thing that I do that would make me feel like I had a 100% day. A Floor action is the thing I can do every day no matter how I feel. I'm going to show up and do this very easy thing every single day. When I think of it that way, I have no choice but to break down my goals into small actionable steps that create a plan for me as I move forward.

Jenny and I had a ceiling every paycheck: write the budget before we got paid, stick to the budget, no spending outside of what was written and lastly, use every bit of variable income on debt. We very rarely hit this goal.

Our floor was to make a big payment on the current debt we were paying off and minimums on payments on all other debts. This was what got us through that entire year.

SMART Goals

SMART goals are goals that are: Specific, Measurable, Achievable, Relevant, and Time-bound.

Specific: What exactly do you want to achieve?

Measurable: How will you track your progress?

Achievable: Is your goal realistic within your current resources?

Relevant: Does this goal align with your larger vision?

Time-bound: What's your timeline for success?

Our specific goal was to pay the debt off in 2 years. We could easily measure it by looking at the numbers. It was achievable and relevant. We had a clear time frame that we wanted to pay the debt off by.

Shrinking that down to actionable steps, we looked at it monthly. Every month the goal was to pay minimums on each debt and throw every bit of extra money at the current smallest debt. We could measure this by writing a budget, sticking to it, and running the numbers weekly, if not daily. For example, if we spent less money on gas than we had budgeted, we sent the leftover money to the current debt. It was very achievable and relevant because we got paid twice a month. Our designated time frame was one month at a time.

This works in every area of your life. Let's say your goal is to improve your communication with your spouse. A SMART plan might look like setting aside 10 minutes daily to check in and actively listen. It's that easy!

Systems or Habit-based Plans

As you execute plans and learn along the way, you begin to discover more about yourself, what truly matters to you, and where you want to go in life. System and habit-based plans work when your internal tools and resources have been refined a bit. These types of plans are built on the person you want to be versus a specific goal. These plans are built for *becoming* versus achieving.

When it came to the debt payoff process, the system planning didn't kick in until six months into the process. As we came into the new year (2021) and did our taxes, we found out we were getting a lot more money due to Covid and child tax credits. I also learned about investing and options trading. Not only did I want to be a person who paid off their debt, I wanted to be a person who saved for retirement, earned a lot of money, set their children up for success, and helped others. I wanted so much more than what Dave was offering me. Thankfully, I found others that approached money differently than Dave Ramsey and the Baby Step Program. This only lit a fire in me to "become" versus just "achieve"; and that's the beauty of the system and habit-based planning. You begin to make moves based on who you want to become, the achieving happens naturally.

Our overall goal was to get out of debt as quickly as possible. We ran the numbers, reran the numbers and ran them again. It was going to take us two years to pay them off using the Debt Snowball. While it was overwhelming to look at two years, we shrank that down to what we could do that day in July of 2020. And the first thing was to save $1000 as quickly as we could. We did. Within a week. We wrote a budget for the next two weeks and officially started our debt payoff process. By simply writing a budget and looking at our numbers, we had flown past step 1 and into step 2 in a matter of a few days. I kept gaining tools and refining how we would tackle this heavy burden. Then, the most important part of making a plan came into place: changing the plan.

Tips for Staying Flexible

Because life is constant, things happen, you get tired, you grow and change, and so will the goals and the plans. We often lock ourselves into "this way" of doing something. I've said it before and I'll say it again, some tools and resources are only good for a certain amount of time. Be aware of that. As the moments come when the old tools no longer serve you, gather new ones and shift your plan accordingly. Stay flexible in how you get to the goal. The person who uses the detour is more likely to get where they want to go faster than the person stuck and complaining.

Pick one small goal and write a SMART plan for it right now. Even if it feels simple, writing it down turns your intention into action.

We constantly updated our plan in the debt payoff process. We quit the Baby Steps and formed our own financial plan. A long-term method that worked for us. And then a year later we changed it all again! The plan is simply A PLAN. It isn't etched in stone. It's all in pencil. Where you want to go and who you want to become will become more refined. How you get there will change over time. Prepare yourself for that and allow yourself the room to grow. Make a plan. A plan isn't just a map; it's your proof that you're capable of turning dreams into action. And every small action brings you closer to your goal.

CHAPTER 4

Practice Consistently

"Success is the sum of small efforts, repeated day in and day out." - Robert Collier

When it comes to life change, most people have the hardest time with this step. While there are many reasons why people stop their life growth process, there's only one way to make change happen. IT HAS TO BE DONE. You must *do* something at some point. Having awareness, gaining tools, making plans, and doing nothing will only bring you anxiety and unnecessary stress. You must do something. Planning sets the stage, but the practice is where the magic happens. And consistency is what turns goals into reality.

Again, most people have no issue starting. Most people have no issue doing something 3 to 4 times. But most people will not keep change going long enough to see any change. And that's why people keep living the lives they've always lived. It's hard to change. And a lot of the time people try to overhaul AND take on tasks they aren't prepared for then fall into a shame/guilt cycle. The key to lasting transformation in your life is practicing consistently.

Practice consistently. That's a weird way to say it. I agree with you. I said it that way on purpose. Because while you are aware of where you are and where you want to go, you have new tools to try, and a plan that makes sense to you, you must change and grow in small intentional steps. So, I call it practice. You're getting accustomed to using these new tools and ideas. You're trying things out. Where most people commit to change, I want you to commit to practicing the tools and practicing consistently. It's the only way things will work out how you want them to.

By taking on small bits and pieces at a time, you can keep working toward your goals and dreams without overwhelming yourself. Take working out as an example. People come in with a goal to lose x amount of weight, or build x amount of muscle, or want to look a certain way by a certain date. Those are big goals. And while they're achievable, I believe that focusing on the habit of showing up when you don't want to is more important to the process than the goal itself.

In the book *Atomic Habits*, author James Clear proposes the idea of the 1% rule. Basically, it says that if you can continuously show up and be 1% better than the day before, time will automatically make you 37% better in a year. The beauty of that is it doesn't take me doing a massive overhaul. All I need to do is practice using the new tools and resources to my advantage every single day. Time will do the rest for me.

Overcoming Resistance to Change

I believe there are 3 things that stop people from staying consistent.

1) Change is hard. Initially, you want to do what's comfortable. You want to stay where you are. The new path is unfamiliar.

When things are uncomfortable or if we don't know if something will work, we don't commit to it fully. And so, we give up.
2) Results don't come quick enough. Because we live in a world where most things happen quickly, we think that should also be the case with our goals and dreams.
3) We wait for the motivation to start or keep going. When we're waiting on an internal tool to kick in that hasn't been developed yet, we quit that much easier.

So how do you overcome these things?

1) Awareness is the biggest ally you have. Having clear goals and dreams that are worth fighting for will change the game for you.
2) Come into this practice knowing you aren't going to see results as quickly as you want. If that's something you can accept before you start, that hurdle doesn't get in the way of the process.
3) Just show up and do it. Do something. Every day. Show up and do something. Make it as easy as possible to do and do it.

Sticking to something every day isn't easy. There will be days when you're tired, distracted, or you just don't want to do it. That's NORMAL. The key is to have strategies ready for those moments. Having awareness, knowing the process will be hard, and showing up and doing the plan regardless of how you feel is the only way to build consistency. Your mind is going to tell you all these things: it's not worth it, you don't want to do it, you can't do it, you don't have enough of this or that, you're not ready, you're tired. So many excuses, and good ones, to stop your progress. But if you can simply practice showing up, the world will be yours sooner than you think.

While there's a battle going on in your mind, there are many ways to help your mind see that things are getting better. Habit trackers are one of my favorite ways to see how I'm doing. By simply marking an X on a calendar or checking off a checklist every day, I can see that I've accomplished something. Immediately you will want the X, the check mark, the completed workout, the healthy meal, the closed ring, the debt paid off, the well-executed budgeted week.

Being able to track the practice you're doing allows you to see how consistent you are. And when you see that you can be consistent, the internal tools of motivation and determination present themselves to you and those become the driving factors for where you want to go and how you get there. Many different habit trackers out there let you visibly see the X mark the spot every day.

Another way is to find an accountability partner. Someone who may have walked the path you want to walk. It could be a coach or a mentor. Finding someone that you can bounce ideas off AND get encouragement from is a massive gift for anyone looking to improve their lives.

You can also try challenges with friends. Weight loss, muscle gain, financial savings challenges, healthy meal challenges, the list goes on and on! Committing to something that gives you a plan while you achieve your goals AND do it with others is a cheat code to attaining every goal you want to reach.

I love the 75 Hard program by Andy Frisela: 2, 45 min workouts (one outside), drink a gallon of water, read 10 pages of a book that helps you achieve your goals, take a picture, and pick a diet of your choice that will aid your workouts. No alcohol or cheat meals. Every day for 75 days. If you miss any part on any given day, you have to start all over again, going back to day 1. While it's very intense and, mostly, an overhaul program, doing it when you're ready with people that are also ready will light a fire in you like never before.

A Story of Daily Practice

In February of 2022, I decided to do this 75 Hard challenge. Mostly because I needed a way to stay consistent in my overall physical health. I began the process afraid. I loved to read, but I really needed to get myself to enjoy working out. My first attempt I got to day 28 and quit because I was upset about an argument with my wife. My second attempt started on August 1st that same year and I completed all 75 days on October 14th. The most interesting things about the process for me were how I had to approach it, my thoughts about working out, and how it changed me forever.

1) Because every day was such an intense day, I was forced to focus on each day as it came. I couldn't think about the 75th day, I could only complete the day I was on. It took this overwhelming program and shrank it into a highly scheduled day for 75 days.

2) I never wanted to do my workout. Not once. While I showed up and completed each workout, I did not want to do it. But what I felt didn't matter compared to the accomplishment I wanted to feel at the end of the program.

3) After that program, I committed to doing SOME SORT of workout every day of my life. Whether it was stretching, free weights, a mile walk, or a full 45-minute HIIT, I was going to do something. And for most of the last 2 years, I've stuck to that.

More important than that story itself was a conversation I had with my dad in the summer of 2022. We were in San Diego at the mall. I was telling him how I didn't want to buy anything because I was between size L and XL. But the XL looked too big on me and the L looked too tight. His advice was to just buy the bigger clothes, so I'd feel better. I refused and told him why. While I had no specific weight goal, I wanted to fit in my clothes, and I wanted to be healthy. That fall, I completed 75 Hard.

Through 2023, I walked most days and did sporadic workouts here and there. In 2024, I committed to complete a one mile walk every day for the year. As the fall of 2024 came around, I had officially slimmed down enough to fit back into my dress pants. I could wear my dress shirts again without them feeling too tight. I completed the goal I had. But more than that, I had proven that taking simple actions every day produce amazing results. Some days all I did was walk. Some days I did 30 minutes of HIIT then walked. Some days I lifted weights. It was all over the place. And the craziest part, all these workouts took place at home in my living room!

Through a dedicated plan to move my body, regardless of what it looked like, I achieved something I never thought was possible. And consistency is what got me there. Everyday. I decided I would show up for myself. Not to look a certain way. Not even to feel a certain way. I did it so I could say I did it.

In the next chapter, we'll talk about changing the plan as you go, but you can never get there if you don't practice consistently. You must build some positive data for yourself to trust and review. And the only way you'll get that data is by doing something. By practicing and practicing consistently. Take the smallest step of your plan and start. You can do this.

What's one small action you can commit to for the next seven days? Write it down and track your progress each day. Start small and build momentum. You don't have to be perfect. You just have to show up. If all you have is 20% and you give that, you gave 100%. Progress isn't about never slipping. It's about choosing to keep going no matter how many times you fall. Just commit.

CHAPTER 5

Learn and Adjust

"The measure of intelligence is the ability to change." - Albert Einstein

The next step in this process is Learn and Adjust. In this step, we simply look at the data we've produced, how we feel about things, what works and doesn't, and we shift our plan accordingly so we can achieve our goals more efficiently.

Flexibility is Freedom

When we begin to change our lives and overhaul old habits, we try "this thing" how others have tried it. We put too much emphasis on what to do versus if it's giving us the results we really want. While we, as humans, are mostly the same, we all have different preferences, likes and dislikes. Some people enjoy challenging themselves with massive tasks. Some people like to keep things as easy as possible. Some people dream big and attack. Some don't. And it's all ok. When it comes to executing your plan, you have to stay flexible and adjust them as you go along. If you wanted to complete 75 Hard, but couldn't lift every day (no one should), then adjust the type of workouts you do. The goal is to complete it. Adjust as you see fit. If you're trying to get your finances in order and Dave Ramsey's Baby Step program seems too overwhelming, slow things down and do what comes easier for you. If you like using budget apps, use apps. If you like using paper and pen, use paper and pen. If you like to track every expense, do that. If you don't, then don't.

Too often people stay locked into a plan that isn't working for them. And when that happens, they start to avoid the goals they wanted to achieve in the first place. But rather than sacrificing the goal, sacrifice the plan. Build a new one. Find new tools. Find better resources. Not only will you keep practicing consistently, but you'll also build confidence in yourself and your overall mindset.

The Gift of Failure and Evaluating Progress

Everyone starts a new process not knowing what it's going to look like. In every process, things are going to happen. You will have pitfalls. You will strike out. You will miss it. Every child learning to walk falls. And they have the best approach, they get back up and try again. That's what you have to do in this process. Failure only means something if it stops you from moving forward. Everyone fails. If you were playing a game and you lost, you failed the point of the game. But if that's all you got from every situation, you'd never change. And that's where course correction comes in. When you inevitably fail, the first thing you have to ask is, "Why?" What happened when this took place? What did I learn from it? How could I approach this differently? Become a course corrector.

By defining yourself as a course corrector, instead of a failure, you continue on a path to life change and growth. Adjusting your plan doesn't mean you failed. It means you're learning, growing, and figuring out what works best for you.

There are multiple ways to do this. I'll give you three.

The first way is mentioned above: check in with yourself. Ask yourself questions. Remember, building awareness is the simple act of gathering information. That's all you're doing: gathering information about the process that you've been practicing consistently. If you don't like the act of working out, but you love feeling better after you work out, adjust the workouts themselves. If tracking the money every day is too overwhelming, but you enjoy knowing where you stand every day, check once or try to check every other day. Adjust the plan, not the goal.

Second, ask for feedback. All of us trust someone. Talk to someone who knows you well and ask if they see any difference in how you are approaching this particular goal. Ask them to give you some feedback from the outside. If you are honest with them, they will be honest with you. And from there, you'll be able to adjust accordingly.

Lastly, check the data. Are you getting the results you want? If so, keep going. If not, adjust until you get the results you want. But this can only happen if you're practicing consistently. You have to give yourself to the process for the data to be there.

I had a client who was working through some issues with her mother. While things were cordial, she kept running into this issue where she wanted to implement boundaries with her mom but couldn't do it without being angry. And she had a very hard time trying to convey these new boundaries to her mother. She came up with a plan: communicate through email only. But the problem with that was she had grown so much and didn't want to cheapen herself or the relationship with her mom. I suggested that she tell her mom she wanted to implement boundaries for the sake of the relationship moving forward versus just letting her mom know she couldn't "do this anymore". It was this slight adjustment of thought that allowed her to relax about what to do next. Further, it allowed her to realize that she was holding out hope for her mother's change and growth. Before this, she could only see her mother as someone that would never change, and she didn't want to be on the receiving end of a toxic relationship. After these changes in approach and realizations, she was able to communicate her wants and needs to her mother without getting angry or feeling dismissed. She was able to have the relationship she wanted while holding her boundaries.

Growth Mindset and Fixed Mindset

When it comes to seeing adjustments as part of the growth process instead of setbacks, it is vital that we have a growth mindset versus a fixed mindset. Allow me to explain what they are and their importance in the process.

Growth mindset is the belief that your abilities, intelligence, and talents can be developed through effort, learning, and perseverance. When you have a growth mindset, you see challenges as opportunities to grow, view feedback as valuable, and are willing to adapt and learn from failures. This shift fosters resilience and continuous improvement.

Fixed Mindset is the belief that your abilities, intelligence, and talents are static traits that cannot be changed. People with a fixed mindset tend to avoid challenges, give up easily when faced with obstacles, and see effort as a sign of inadequacy. They often fear failure because it feels like a reflection of their identity, rather than an opportunity to grow. Remember the client who didn't want to become self-aware because she didn't want to be selfish? She was stuck in a fixed mindset.

A growth mindset is vital to the "learn and adjust" part of the Simple Shift Method. Something is going to challenge you every day. Something will not go quite as planned. Something is going to be a little harder than you thought it would be. And when these moments come, you need to be in a place mentally to see it happening and prepare to adjust.

To do that, keep your goals in mind. Write them down and keep them visible. When things get hard, having the vision written and visible keeps your focus on where it should be. When we were paying off the debt, I wrote things on my vision board and taped it to my bathroom mirror. Not only did I have encouragement written on there, but I also wrote messages specifically for my mindset. Things like, "I know you don't want to do this; we have no other choice.", "Yes, this is hard. That's ok", "One day at a time, slow down." These things kept me sane when I felt like giving up.

Remind yourself that the adjustments are taking you one step closer to the thing you're trying to achieve. Whenever a plan gets refined, I get excited. This means I learned something, tried it and it didn't work. Because of that process, I can now rule something out and with refined focus, keep moving toward what I want.

Every single adjustment you make is bringing you closer to becoming a growth machine. It also builds confidence in the things you take on. While the next thing may not work, some of it may work. There may be a small piece of another process that stays with you forever. You just don't know. But you will be able to keep going. And that's the beauty of learning and adjusting. Schedule a 10-minute check in at the end of the week. Think about the last 7 days and the plan you committed to. Ask yourself: What went well? What could I improve? What's one adjustment I can make for next week?

Don't be afraid of letting go and changing. That's the point of it all: to keep growing. Life will always throw curveballs. Every adjustment you make is a testament to your resilience and your commitment to creating the life you deserve.

CHAPTER 6

Evolve Continuously

"Be not afraid of growing slowly, be afraid only of standing still." - Chinese Proverb

---

Evolve Continuously. What does that even mean? It means you become a person chasing lifelong growth. We may know a lot about a lot of things, but we don't know everything, and we never will. While some people hear that and get discouraged, I hear that and feel free to find as many things as I can to learn.

Every person on earth is living a different life than you are. Everyone has something to share with the next person. But if you never look to see the beauty, lesson, tool or resource that is before you, you'll miss every golden nugget that crosses your path. Evolving continuously will automatically make you a person who invites growth in every area of your life. It changes you. This is where the internal tools (motivation, confidence, discipline, self-control, authenticity) gain their power. The quicker you realize there's so much to learn and use for yourself, the quicker you live the life you want to live.

Avoiding Complacency

As you move through life achieving different goals, you'll begin to find yourself looking for the dopamine hit of achieving goals. The reason this step is part of the Simple Shift process is because goals will only get you so far. After we achieve them, we take our foot off the gas and rest a little longer than we want. Or worse, we fall back into the habits we had before we started the process. But if you can keep looking to improve and learn, it sharpens the dreams that you have. It fine-tunes the person you want to become. Learning and improving become more about who you are versus what you do.

Once this version of you kicks in, you become unstoppable. You begin to believe that you can achieve every dream in your heart. And it's a beautiful thing! I want to emphasize here: evolving continuously doesn't mean constantly striving. It means staying curious and building on your progress! Having a growth mindset makes this very attainable along the way. Instead of saying 'this is just how things are', you'll begin asking 'what can I learn from this?'

Practical Steps to Keep Growing

At every stage in life and life change, there are ways to keep evolving.

1) Reading books. The fact you're holding this and reading it is going to give you tools you may not have had before. It may clarify some goals and dreams. It may give you encouragement that you need to keep going or to take the next step. Reading is one of the greatest tools we are all capable of using to keep learning and growing. My favorite thing about books: You don't need to take every word from the book and apply it to your life. Read the whole thing, take

what you need for your goals and dreams and throw the rest away.

2) Challenge yourself. Try new things. Take on challenges on purpose. what you will find is this: life's challenges aren't that bad if you're placing challenges on yourself. Conversations are easier to have. Regulating your emotions gets easier. Managing your money becomes easier. Taking on challenges will change and grow you into a person you never saw coming.

3) Find a coach. While you may be aware of yourself, we all need an outside perspective to help us with our blind spots. When that happens with people we trust, they challenge us in the best ways. We can become the people we want to be that much faster because we have someone on our side gently challenging us and encouraging us to greatness.

When my wife and I first started paying our debt off, I knew very little about investing and options trading. Over the last four years, I have read many books on money mindset, business, and negotiations. As of this writing, I am on the brink of signing the biggest contract of my life (so far) to offer mindset coaching for a company in Southern California.

My favorite part about planning my budget for the future was how concerned I was with investing my money for myself, my wife, and my children. I want every person in my immediate family to have little to no financial worries. I want my children to be able to live their lives from 18-30 with no worries about student loans or down payments for homes. My biggest concern is taking the financial burden off them so they can live and dream and attack life with as much vigor as they can stand. If I had not continued to learn what was financially possible, I would've stopped at debt payoff process and that would've been it. My money would sit in a checking or savings account and waste away. Instead, I have so many dreams that are not only possible but are very easy to make happen because of who I am today and the learning I've done over the years.

And it isn't just my finances. I feel this way with my physical health. My business. My friendships. My marriage. My parenting. Because I'm constantly learning and growing, I feel so equipped for the life I want to live. There's no other feeling like this. Knowing the life you want to live, how you're getting there, and adjusting along the way, makes you someone who becomes unstoppable.

When you take a growth mindset into every situation you find yourself in, you keep becoming a better version of yourself. "Hard" issues become challenges you know you'll overcome. You may not have the tools at the moment, but you have confidence that you will find them, use them, and create a way forward. Keep growing. Keep trying. Keep learning. There's so much out there that you haven't come across yet. And so much of it will make you a better person for it. Even now, take some time to look back at the last six months or the last year. What's one thing you've improved in that time frame? Take the time to celebrate your progress! You have hard proof that you can keep growing already! When you keep growing, you don't just change your life, you inspire change in the lives of those around you as well.

Keep growing.

CHAPTER 7

The Power of the SIMPLE Shift

"Go confidently in the direction of your dreams. Live the life you have imagined." - Henry David Thoreau

The SIMPLE Shift Method

See the Challenge - Build awareness. Who are you currently? Where do you want to go? Who do you want to be? Where are you right now? Answering these questions sets everything in motion.

Identify Tools and Resources - After building awareness and seeing the challenge, you must gather tools for this journey. What tools do you already have? What tools do you need? This step is not exhaustive, it is simple. Get 2-3 new tools to try then make a plan.

Make a Plan - Using the tools you have; how will you approach this? How will you get to the place you want? How can you best use these tools? Then make a statement: I will do x on this day and time until x happens.

Practice Consistently - Do it. *Put the rubber to the road, put your money where your mouth is, put the pedal to the metal.* Whatever phrase you want to use, you gotta make a move. You have to start. commit to trying the new tools on your specified time frame.

Learn and Adjust - As you build data, check in with yourself. Find out what's working and what isn't. Give yourself grace to change the plan, to find new tools, to keep refining. Develop a growth mindset. Gather information about the process and course correct.

Evolve Continuously - Keep growing. Every day is another day to become the person you want to be. Don't shy away from this step. You are well on your way to becoming a growth machine.

Awareness sparks the shift. Tools and resources equip you for what's ahead. A plan focuses your efforts. Consistency solidifies the change. Adjustments refine it. And continuous evolution ensures the transformation lasts a lifetime.

The best part about using the Simple Shift Method for one part of your life is that it will automatically ripple into other areas of your life. Once you see how easy it is to overcome "the impossible things", the last step of the process will push you to improve other parts of your life.

Success Stories

For me, this entire process started with the money. As I became a different person regarding our money and money habits, I wanted to see if it could help me with working out and eating healthier. Before I knew it, I had gained new tools, read a couple of books and then I was completing the 75 Hard challenge. That process then led me to challenge my emotional health.

I found myself getting angry with others if I thought they weren't accepting my unsolicited advice. And when that happened, I would cut people off. I couldn't let things go. It wasn't ok and the process started all over again. I built awareness, gained tools (emotional words), which led me to name my emotions, which led to emotional regulation, which led to a better handle on my communication in my friendships and relationships. I became a new person all over again. And as I continued to evolve, the emotional journey pushed me in my spiritual journey and relationship with Jesus. I wanted to have everything Jesus said He came to give me. So, I read and studied and applied everything the red letters told me. Life opened up in a brand-new way. As I read books, watched sermons, and listened to podcasts, I "leveled up" again. That led to being a better husband, which led to becoming a better father. The journey has continued, and this process has helped me over and over again. All due to a simple shift of my money habits in July of 2020.

I had a client, Monica, who had been talking about moving from her small town in New Mexico to a bigger city in another state for years. For about 3-4 years she talked about moving "at some point". While the idea would come and go, it was always there but seemed too out of reach. Eventually, a lack of clarity and accomplishment led her to a place of depression. In December of 2023, Monica was at her lowest. As we were talking one night, I told her to start doing something. Just to wake up and have a checklist that she could say she accomplished SOMETHING every day. Within a week of that conversation, she took the simple shift of committing to making her bed, walking a mile, and being silly in the mirror for a certain amount of time (she had been taking herself too seriously) every day. While she embarked on this process, it took her 14 days to come back to life. Suddenly, she had energy again. She was laughing again. She was dreaming of what could be again. An opportunity presented itself for her to move with friends to Los Angeles a month later. Because of the work she had put in over the previous five weeks, she was not only able to think about it and speak from a place of peace, but she accepted and began to make plans and set herself up for that move.

Mark was a client who told me he knew what he needed to do, but he said, "I just don't feel like doing it. So, I don't". When we started his awareness journey, he could barely dream. He didn't know what he wanted. He didn't know who he wanted to be. And therefore, he had no plan to get there. As we talked, I challenged him to live as the person he wanted to be proud of in six months. I gave him basic steps to take: sleep in the bed with his wife, gratitude lists, name his emotions, slow down, use "I" statements (statements that convey what he feels and desires). Over the next six weeks, Mark went from telling me how he had no motivation to do anything to telling me that he was capable of achieving! Not only that, he realized that he knew he would fail, but even that was ok as long as he kept getting up and pressing toward the person he wanted to become. My favorite part about Mark's process was the fact that he was proud of himself in six weeks when he thought it would take six months. All it took was simplifying his life, his dreams, his approach and the steps to get there. He's a different person and that only came from changing the game for himself.

Tina was a married, stay-at-home mom who decided to homeschool her children. When she made this decision she was already overwhelmed by a lack of schedule, usually moving too quickly, and trying to appease any and everyone. With a vague idea of what she wanted to do; she quickly became stressed by how many homeschooling ideas were out there. This negatively compounded onto her gym life, her work schedule, her marriage, and friendships.

When we started working together, I gave her the simple tools of slowing down and telling the truth. With these two tools, it changed so many facets of her life. She began to slow down when it came to her parenting, noticing her own emotions and reactions. She began to slow down and be honest about her work life. She began to slow down and ask her husband for the direct help she needed at different times of the day. She slowed down in her friendships and began being honest about what activities she could and couldn't do. In committing to slowing down, so many things in Tina's life changed. While it took the better part of a year, the immediate results kept pushing her to follow through with slowing down and being honest in the next situation. It was beautiful to see her thrive as in every role she had, but most importantly, as a person.

For every single one of us, it comes down to the same thing: one simple shift at a time. One shift will naturally cross over into other parts of life.

Encouragement

Here's what I want you to remember:

- **You are not stuck.** Every small step forward moves you closer to the life you want.
- **You are not alone.** Others have walked this path before, and they've made it. So can you.
- **You are worthy of change.** The life you dream of isn't too big or too far out of reach. It's waiting for you to claim it.

Your Life Can Look Different

Imagine your life a year from now. Imagine what could happen if you started making small shifts today. You don't have to imagine drastic transformations—just picture yourself feeling more in control, more confident, and more at peace. Picture the ripple effect of those shifts spreading into your relationships, your work, and your sense of purpose.

Now imagine what happens if you don't start. A year from now, will you still be stuck in the same patterns, wishing for something more? Or will you look back and thank yourself for taking that first step?

The choice is yours. And I believe you'll make the choice to shift. Because deep down, you already know you're capable of it.

A Final Word

Before we close, I want to say thank you. Thank you for showing up. Thank you for trusting this process. Thank you for investing in yourself. Writing this book has been an honor, but the real work, the real magic—that's in your hands now.

So, here's my final encouragement: Start today. Don't wait for the perfect moment or the perfect plan. Just take one small step. Trust the process. Lean into the discomfort. And know that every single shift, no matter how small, is moving you closer to the life you deserve.

You can do this. I believe in you. Now it's time to believe in yourself.

Your simple shift starts now. Let's go.

The Simple Shift Method in Action

Now that you've read the book and explored the Simple Shift Method, it's time to put it into action. The only thing left to do is pick a challenge—big or small—and begin the process. To help you take that first step, I've included a set of questions designed to guide you through each stage of the method. These questions will help you uncover what's holding you back, identify the resources you need, and take practical steps toward your goal. Whether it's improving a relationship, tackling a personal habit, or chasing a dream, this process will walk you through seeing the challenge, making shifts, and transforming your life, one intentional step at a time. Let's get started!

SEE THE CHALLENGE

What is the challenge you want to overcome?

1. What specific situation or obstacle are you facing right now?
2. How long has this challenge been affecting you?
3. Why do you feel this is important to address now?
4. What impact has this challenge had on your daily life or relationships?
5. What would your life look like if this challenge were resolved?

What thoughts or feelings come up when you think about this challenge?

1. What emotions are strongest when you think about this challenge?
2. Do these emotions motivate or discourage you? Why?
3. Are there any fears or doubts that arise when facing this challenge?
4. How does your self-talk change when thinking about this situation?
5. What positive feelings might come from resolving this challenge?

IDENTIFY TOOLS AND RESOURCES

What tools or resources do you already have that could help you with this challenge?

1. What personal strengths (e.g., skills, habits, or knowledge) can you use?
2. Who in your life (e.g., friends, family, mentors) could support you?
3. What past experiences have prepared you to handle this challenge?
4. Are there any tools (e.g., books, apps, or strategies) you've used successfully before?
5. What makes you confident that you have the ability to overcome this?

What additional tools or resources might you need to find or create to address this challenge?

1. What skills or knowledge do you feel are missing right now?
2. Who could you reach out to for advice, mentorship, or help?
3. Are there any books, courses, or tools you could explore for support?
4. What actions could you take to create the resources you need?
5. How will you ensure that you consistently use these new resources?

MAKE A PLAN

What is one small, actionable step you can take today to begin addressing this challenge?

1. What is the simplest thing you can do right now to start moving forward?
2. Does this step feel manageable and achievable? Why or why not?
3. How can you set aside time or resources to make this step happen today?
4. Who can help hold you accountable for completing this step?
5. How will you celebrate or acknowledge this progress once it's done?

PRACTICE CONSISTENTLY

How can you commit to practicing this new step consistently?

1. What specific time of day or routine will include this new practice?
2. How will you track your progress to stay motivated?
3. What obstacles might get in the way of consistency, and how can you handle them?
4. Who can encourage or check in with you to stay on track?
5. How will practicing this consistently change your perspective over time?

LEARN AND ADJUST

What's working, and what's not working?

1. What results have you seen since you started addressing this challenge?
2. Are there parts of your approach that feel easy and effective? Why?
3. What parts of your approach feel hard or unhelpful?
4. How have your feelings or thoughts about the challenge changed?
5. What feedback from others (if any) could help you improve your process?

What adjustments can you make to improve your approach?

1. What's one thing you could do differently starting tomorrow?
2. Are there tools or strategies you haven't tried yet but want to?
3. How can you simplify or streamline your process to make it easier?
4. Is there anyone you need to ask for feedback or advice?
5. What mindset shifts could help you approach this challenge with fresh energy?

EVOLVE CONTINUOUSLY

How has your perspective, approach, or situation evolved since you started this process?

1. What have you learned about yourself during this journey?
2. How has your confidence grown since you began addressing this challenge?
3. What changes have you noticed in your daily life or relationships?
4. How has your understanding of the challenge itself evolved?
5. What would you tell your past self about this process?

What's the next small shift you can make to continue improving in this area?

1. What's one thing you're excited to work on next?
2. How will this next step build on what you've already done?
3. What will success look like for this next shift?
4. Who or what will support you as you take this next step?
5. How can you keep celebrating the small wins along the way?

Acknowledgements

I'm gonna keep this simple because the list will get very long, very fast.

Jenny, my wife. I love you. Thank you for being you.

My children, thank you for being my greatest challenge and blessing simultaneously.

To my Mom and Dad. Thank you for every piece of life you have given me.

My Day 1's. This is just the beginning.

My Day 2's. Yeesh. I love yall forever man. Let's go on vacation!

To find more information about Simple Shifts scan the QR code.

You can also find Rafer on Facebook, Instagram and Youtube: @raferowensjr

Made in the USA
Las Vegas, NV
18 March 2025